Finding Joy

Finding Joy

THE YEAR APART
THAT MADE ME A BETTER WIFE

Hope N. Griffin

AMBASSADOR INTERNATIONAL
GREENVILLE, SOUTH CAROLINA & BELFAST, NORTHERN IRELAND

www.ambassador-international.com

Finding Joy:
The Year Apart that Made Me a Better Wife

© 2015 by Hope N. Griffin
All rights reserved

ISBN: 978-1-62020-537-2
eISBN: 978-1-62020-467-2

Cover Design and Page Layout by Hannah Nichols
eBook Conversion by Anna Riebe Raats

AMBASSADOR INTERNATIONAL
Emerald House
427 Wade Hampton Blvd.
Greenville, SC 29609, USA
www.ambassador-international.com

AMBASSADOR BOOKS
The Mount
2 Woodstock Link
Belfast, BT6 8DD, Northern Ireland, UK
www.ambassadormedia.co.uk

The colophon is a trademark of Ambassador

There is a temptation on my first book to list every person who has brought me to this point. There are so many who have made this journey with me. Those who cried with us at our daughter's diagnoses and helped us in immeasurable ways, my military sisters as we held each other up during deployments and still do, my friends who prayed for me and encouraged me through my crisis of faith, and those who were positioned in certain unforgettable, life-changing moments. There are just so many to thank. But there is only one who has held my hand, or dreamed of holding it, through this entire journey. Without his support, love, and occasional arguments for material, there would be no book. From the moment we met, he has been my encourager, my strength when I have none. To my best friend, my favorite. John Griffin, this book is for you.

CONTENTS

PART 1

Pre-Deployment

CHAPTER 1

Dear John

FOR THE FIRST FEW YEARS, I anticipated orders to move. I waited anxiously. The day we arrived at Fort Bliss, I was ready to leave. When my husband joined the military, the one thing I was excited about were the moves every two to three years. I love uprooting. I've never before planted roots. Discovering new places, people, and opportunities thrilled me. Now we have been here over six years. I have lived here longer than I have lived anywhere else in my life.

Today, I find myself in new territory. I am content. I am deeply planted.

I have no desire to go anywhere. I have found my place. I have a job I love with abundant opportunities attached. My youngest was born here. She is my desert baby and knows only the dry, dusty air of El Paso. My older two have finally adapted and no longer call the jack rabbits kangaroos. I no longer notice the constant layer of dust on the windowsills or the whistle of the wind as it arranges our patio furniture. They have transformed from minor annoyances to familiar friends.

When we first moved here, I found myself empathizing with the Israelites as they wandered the desert in discontent. My needs were met, yet I desired something richer than manna. I complained. I learned to distrust FRG (Family Readiness Groups) and fear deployments. Housing was a source of contention, and neighbors were only neighborly when they had needs. I withdrew.

Now I sit here, fully engaged with the culture of El Paso. I know which restaurants to avoid and the best ones to frequent. I can even tell you what was located in a building three businesses before the current one. It used to be when I ventured out, I could complete every errand without seeing one familiar face. Now it is impossible to go on one without running into a friend. I am engaged in the lives around me.

So it should come as no surprise when I overhear my soldier telling his father that we are moving.

He has been trying to tell me for two weeks now, and every time he has brought it up, I simply respond, "Not until orders are in hand." Or "The Army will change its mind." I have an until-boots-are-on-the-ground mentality. We've been told Germany and Japan in the past, and I've jumped in heart first only to be shot down. But there is something different in the way he is speaking. He is making plans. Setting dates. Mapping it out in his head. And I want to stomp my feet deeper into the ground, hold on tight to the roots I've let burrow in, and fight to stay. I am content. So naturally, it is time to go.

* * *

I first took John home to my family under the pretense that my father would find something wrong with him and give me an excuse not to date him. John and I had met not long after I had ended a very tumultuous four-year relationship in which my parents disapproved, and rightly so. I was broken. Yet there was something about this man that I could not walk away from.

When we met, I had thrown myself into my studies, no time for friends and definitely not distractions. I had tried and failed to discourage him. He pursued. Out of excuses, I handed him my scheduling book and told him to pencil himself in. He did.

John first met my parents at a Chinese restaurant on the edge of Hot Springs, AR. The evening became more of an intervention from family insistent that I lighten up and give the world at large a chance. I was cynical, broken, and determined to regain control of my life. The universe that communicates through fortune cookies had other plans. It encouraged John, "Rome was not built in a day. Be patient." He still carries the crumpled reminder in his wallet.

* * *

I am not an easy person to love. I know this because of the difficulty I have in loving myself. There is the need for perfectionism in myself that I am unable to obtain. Accepting God's grace while struggling with guilt has often plagued me. In my head, I know the verses. I know the free gift of grace. In my heart, I wrestle with the fact that I am undeserving. I want to earn what I take.

* * *

I love hearing about how others met. They are usually much kinder to each other than I was to John.

My grandparents, John and Lee Turner, met on a train during World War II. John was with a fellow soldier, and Lee was headed home with a friend from school. John looked across the train and saw this beautiful girl and just couldn't walk away. The two soldiers sat down across from Lee and her friend. They played card games and talked the length of the train ride. When it was time to part, John gave Lee his pocket watch, asking her to count the minutes until he returned to her. And she did.

I love their story. But John and Lee's romance did not come without pain. When Lee met John, she had already lost her fiancé to the war. Here stood another soldier asking her to love him, to wait for him. And she chose to. She chose to go through the pain of not hearing from her love for months, to receive the occasional letter (no phone calls or Skype), and to wait anxious long nights holding his watch and wondering if he would ever return. Then one night, she received the dreaded familiar knock at her door. John was gone. MIA. His plane, in which he was a ball turret gunner, was missing.

For days she grieved him, fearful he would not return. Then one day there was another knock at her door, and there he stood. In the end, they were married till death took them from us, survived by three children, seven grandchildren, and an ever increasing number of great grandchildren.

I met my John while working at Olive Garden. He was a waiter and line cook, and I was a hostess. Within a year we were engaged, moving to Dallas so I could start grad school, and a year after that, married.

Before we ever met, John had served a year in the Army and had then been a cop before heading into the exciting world of food service. I never expected the direction he would go. I was prepared at any moment for him to present the desire to rejoin the police force. He had served for five years, and I knew he missed it. What I wasn't prepared for was, at the age of 35 with two children and soon to discover a third on the way, that my John would present and actively pursue reenlistment.

John had struggled in the volatile world of food management. At the time this crazy notion of the Army popped into his brain, he was an assistant manager at Chili's and taking EMT classes toward his dream of being an ER doctor. A long stretch lay before him. I was busy working for Fellowship of Christian Athletes and running a home-based business on the side. John mentioned the Army in passing, and I brushed him off thinking he was insane, would never pass the physical, that it was just a pipe dream. Little did I know. Within only a few months, our second child was diagnosed with a rare form of cancer, and we were thrown into a whirlwind of doctor's visits, trips to St. Jude in Memphis, and an emotional tailspin. I worked solely from home during this time and had difficulty putting in the hours. Our financial situation became dire. John quit his EMT classes, and we moved into a smaller home where we just got stuck.

John started talking about the Army again but this time more seriously. I thought it was just about money, so I put in as many hours as I could, tried to up my sales, and took on a freelance writing job. Turns out it was about a lot more than money—you never go into the Army for the money!

John enlisted because it is who he is. It offered an opportunity to pursue his dream of college. It gave him the avenue to serve others and his country. He wanted to give his life for something greater than himself, for an ideal of what this country was founded on.

But I thought he was running away. Running from our toddler's cancer, running from our inability to communicate, running from our financial desperation. I was wrong.

I was the one running.

DISCUSSION QUESTIONS

1. How did you meet your spouse?

2. Was his career path a mutual decision? Was he already on this path before you met him?

3. Do you find yourself content where you are, or do you want more? Why do you think you feel that way?

CHAPTER 2

Pre-Deployment

ONE MONTH BEFORE JOHN DEPLOYED, we sat down and watched a movie together called *One Night with the King* (Sajbel 2006). I have always been fascinated with Esther, her grace and beauty, her triumph amongst those who despised her people. Esther is about a young woman who is captured and forced into a beauty competition to become King Xerxes' queen. For one year, she prepares for one night.

One year.

One year.

Esther's one year is described in only six verses found in Esther 2:8–14. For ONE year in order to spend ONE night with one of the most insane kings in history, Esther prepared herself. "For in this way they had to fulfill their time of cosmetic treatment: six months with oil of myrrh, and six months with perfume and various ointments used by women" (Esther 2:12b NET).

One year is the exact amount of time my husband would be gone. One year of beauty treatments for Esther . . . hey, how about one year to beautify me! Isn't my husband worth that? Aren't I worth that?

Suddenly a year apart didn't seem so long when I had the excitement of lavender baths, facials, and pedicures ahead of me.

Unlike John and myself, Esther didn't volunteer for her role. Rather, she was forced into participating in King Xerxes' beauty pageant and was thrust into a year of beauty treatments, being waited on by eunuchs and soaked in perfume in order to spend one night of passion with the king. And the prize? If she is good in the sack, King Xerxes will choose her for his queen; if not, he may never call for her again, and she will spend the rest of her life in the harem—no husband, no children, no future.

Esther was snatched with other young women throughout the province of Susa and relocated to the Royal Harem. Her world was changed from the quiet Jewish home of her cousin Mordecai to the women's quarters of a pagan palace.

From the moment she was born, she began to wait. There was so much the world required and so little she could offer. She waited by the graveside of her parents, at the table of her cousin who became her caregiver, she waited in a country not her own, she waited as men chose her fate, she waited with the other women as one by one they entered the bedroom of the king, she waited her whole life. Humility and wisdom permeated her wait. And at just the right moment in time, she was shown her purpose and she saved a nation.

The book of Esther can be read in less than an hour, though the story spans years of waiting for God to show up. It is a story of loneliness, desire, determination, and purpose. It is a story not unlike our own.

John was snatched from my world. Yes, we volunteered. Yes, we knew it was coming. But in my heart, I felt him ripped from home and relocated half a world away. A year felt so very long. An eternity lay between Novembers.

NOTHING is the same.

Only our past, who we are, is with us, and suddenly we realize that is not enough. I can dwell momentarily or for hours and days on what we had before he left, yet it isn't always enough. I want desperately to hold him, to feel his hand in mine, his hot breath whispering in my ear. Instead, separated by an ocean and a war, I get momentary glances at a face that is quickly changing from things I am unable to comprehend.

The question that haunts me? "Are we strong enough for what lies ahead?"

I find solace with other military wives. Comfort in the fact they have done this numerous times before. Joy in our fellowship, strength in their moments of weakness, and weakness in their moments of strength. We sharpen one another and supply the support necessary to face a year.

My son said goodbye to his best friend yesterday. It seems as if we are always saying goodbye. Even with the use of Skype and FaceTime, it still is not the same as sitting in a room sharing Legos or running through the neighborhood with Nerf guns. He is heartbroken.

Today he chose to spend the day with me. To sit in my office, to run around doing errands, to drive to the other side of El Paso and back, all because he did not want to sit at home missing his friend. As we pulled out of the last parking lot and headed home, I could tell the fake happy he had showcased all day was dissipating. So when he asked for my phone, I willingly handed it over.

"Siri, what's the fastest way home?" I hear from the back seat.

A sense of joy came over Ian as he began to give me blow-by-blow directions for the return trip while calling out restaurants and businesses that were on his map that were slightly out of view from our travel path. The next thirty minutes of an otherwise boring day became an adventure. He was in control, and the world around him made sense.

Despite the world around us, despite the fact that our soldiers leave on multiple deployments, despite the fact that we struggle with loneliness, depression, a lack of control, and soldiers who return to us many times broken (whether in spirit or physically), despite all of this, we can live full, happy lives. By doing so we will change the world around us, and we will bring joy to our children and friends and strength to our soldier while away and upon their return.

DISCUSSION QUESTIONS

1. If you were given a year and unlimited resources, what would you do to improve you?

2. Read Esther 2:1–14. What type of beauty treatments did these women undergo and why?

3. Read Ecclesiastes 4:9–10. Do you have a battle buddy picked out for this deployment? Battle buddies are like accountability partners whose spouses are also deployed. They let you know when you've stayed in your pajamas too many weeks in a row, help you flee the negativity, encourage you to hit the gym, and cry with you over ice cream on those exceptionally difficult days. Make a list of what qualities you would like in a battle buddy and then go find one. Stick with her through good and bad times.

4. What are you looking forward to during this time apart? Is there a project or a goal you have been putting off? A road trip to take or a degree to pursue?

PART 2

What Living Apart Looks Like

CHAPTER 3

Does Anyone Know a Eunuch for Hire?

ON NOVEMBER 21, MY HUSBAND left for Iraq and I, for all intents and purposes, planned to begin "The Esther Project" on November 22. As a mother I have been reminded over and over that plans never happen and life is only as pleasant as my ability to wing it. Biting back my own tears as John told me to leave because the goodbyes were taking too long, I pried my daughter from my husband's arms and then from the fence we passed and also the car door as I tried to cram her into her car seat, all while struggling with the other two. As we pulled away from the buses and other crying families, my children pleaded with me to take them to Grandma right then and there. We didn't leave for Grandma's house for three days, or was it a week . . . I quickly realized that in order to have a year of beauty treatments, it would require the presence of my own personal eunuch, which I can honestly say I don't know where to find.

The first two months passed with a haze around them of trying to remember to pay each bill, which day was trash day (even though I had regularly criticized him for never remembering), and learning that my husband did more than just sit in front of the TV or tinker on the computers. All his tinkering, it turned out, wasn't out of fun but out of a necessity to keep our electronics alive. By month 3, there were two broken VCRs, a laptop that wouldn't turn on, another that wouldn't stay on, a desktop with a broken sound card, a freezer that died and bled red popsicle, a sunroof that refused to close, bill collectors who did not like my new methods, problems with the car that the dealership refused to cover on our warranty until they got a phone call from my husband in Iraq, and the list goes on. In addition to trying to keep up with my normal pre-deployment schedule with 5-year-old, 3-year-old, and 1-year-old children, I had taken the advice "stay busy" to a new extreme and added online school, teaching two Bible studies, T-ball, judo, tap and ballet, and volunteering at the church. In addition, there was my sister's wedding in Florida requiring a 3-day road trip there and back with the above mentioned children, and my daughter's doctor visits at St. Jude in Memphis that occur every 3 months.

Of course, with children, there are little everyday changes that alter the course of your life. Right when I thought I had this deployment thing figured out, the kids on a schedule, and life calm enough to start my very coveted "Esther Project," things changed.

The day after Easter, headed into month 5 of the deployment, I thought I had it figured out, but my children knew better.

What a day!

First it was Ian, the 5-year-old, screaming from the tub. "MOM! MOM! Alex pooped in the tub!"

Alexis is the 17-month-old and was not even in the bathroom, let alone in the tub.

"Ian, don't fib. You pooped in the tub, not your sister."

"No, Mom, really it wasn't me; it was Alex. Look."

Sure enough, there was a nice gift and a nice smear along the outside of the tub. But Alex was standing by me at this point, completely clothed and not a drop of water on her. Though Ian continued to insist it was his little sister who left me the treat.

As I made my disgusted why-did-you-do-this face and got ready to clean, Ian burst into laughter.

"Mom, Alex did it, but it's chocolate!"

Sure enough, Alex had emptied one of her Easter eggs filled with dark chocolate balls into the bath water, and Ian had played his first prank ever on his mom. At least one of us was enjoying a luxurious chocolate bath.

Not much later, I had deposited all three children at the kitchen table to color quietly while I tried to steal a few minutes to shower. I thought a mid-morning shower was the perfect way to jump start my "Esther Project." I pulled out my unwind salts and scented body wash.

Right as I sudsed up, Ian came running in. "Mom! Katie is stuck on top of the car!"

Katie is my 3-year-old. At this point, I'm not believing the little boy who cried wolf.

"Sure, Ian," I said as I added a nice thick slathering of shampoo to my hair.

"No really, Mom, come on; she's stuck!"

So, covered in soap, without my glasses, and completely blind, I grabbed my very thin bath robe and ran to the kitchen. The only one there was Alex, still strapped into her booster seat coloring. Out the back door I ran to find Katie sitting on top of the car, a little scared but smiling. She had looked out the window to see an abandoned Easter basket on top of the car and decided to be a hero and rescue it. The basket was rescued, but she was stuck. So, in all my sudsy glory,

I rescued the three-year-old and returned to finish a five-second shower. Hopefully none of my neighbors saw a thing.

A few hours later, as I'm folding laundry, completely having given up on pampering myself, Ian once again comes running.

"Mom! Alex is on top of the bunk bed!"

"Uh huh." I turned back to my laundry.

"No, mom, she climbed the side and is up top. Come see."

Sprinting to the bedroom and raising my gaze to the top bunk, I saw my 17-month-old, who was too afraid to stand on playground equipment, running laps back and forth, giggling uncontrollably. *Great*, I thought. *She can't climb out of her crib yet, but she can scale a bunk bed with no ladder. My life just changed forever.*

That night I packed all of my scented soaps and luxurious pampering items back into their rarely opened Tupperware container and put them back under the sink. The idea of using them anytime soon was absurd. I could only hope my deodorant was strong enough to handle the showerless days I envisioned ahead.

Beauty treatments? I did good to wash my face and brush my teeth every night before dropping into bed. I needed one of Esther's eunuchs, a personal maintenance man, chef, and just plain superman. Or maybe just Super Nanny.

When I had first looked at the year ahead, it had been about taking care of my outer beauty to prepare myself for John's return. What really needed a good dose of perfume was my inward being.

At six months, it was easier to look back and see who I was when he left, who I was becoming (which wasn't pleasant), and who I truly wanted to be.

One thing I knew for sure: I was lonely and unhappy.

In *Much Ado About Loving*, Jack Murnighan speaks of loneliness as a "sadness [that] makes the joys sweeter, just as the fleeting life span of the mayfly makes its struggles and beauty that much more exquisite; it may live but an hour, but it will do so aloft" (Murnighan 2012, 19). It is when we know of loss that we can truly appreciate the beauty of what we have. It is spending a year of not having that makes me smile when I trip over the boots he leaves by the front door or the sight of the dirty uniform balled up in the bedroom corner.

But the truth about loneliness as we are experiencing it? It makes us vulnerable. Satan has permeated our world with so many lies. There are things that Satan would never dream to tempt us with until we are at our most vulnerable. When jealousy first reared its ugly head, God warned Cain that "sin is crouching at the door. It desires to dominate you, but you must subdue it" (Genesis 4:7b NET). Sin lies in wait, just as it did in the garden, looking for the opportune time to strike. It tricks us into believing the world's lie that, at our core, mankind is inherently good. Sin takes us off guard, corners us, and waves temporary fixes, false healing for our hurt, and blinds us from the consequences. At its very nature, sin deceives. It waits patiently.

We are inundated with images of happy couples in the media. Some of them are married, some of them found each other while married to others, some of them have no desire to ever commit, but all of them are happier than the lonely military spouse who is pining away for a partner half a world away who may or may not come home, and even if he or she does, they won't be coming home the same. And sin sits back and waits patiently, tossing the forbidden fruit from hand to hand, looking for that perfect moment to catch us in our most vulnerable moment. Days go by without hearing from our soldier, and our heads fill with worries of unfaithfulness or death, and temptation attacks.

When I think of military spouses in the Bible, the first one that always jumps out at me is Bathsheba and her Jody. Yes, I just called King David a Jody because, well, for a moment in history, he was. (If you've not heard of the term, a Jody is someone who stays home from war and sleeps with a soldier's girlfriend or spouse.[1]) Bathsheba's husband was away at war while his commander, the king, stayed home. One night when the king could not sleep, he went to his rooftop to admire his kingdom—and lo and behold, he spied a woman bathing on her rooftop. Now David, who should have been at war with every other able-bodied man in Israel, was standing on his roof in the dusk of evening while Bathsheba bathed herself in what she believed to be a safe place. Her curves caught David's eye, and he immediately inquired of her, learned that her husband was away at war, and summoned her to his palace.

I believe there is a Bathsheba in each and every one of us. We go about our daily lives doing our best to wait for our husbands, but there are predators all around who seek to destroy our marriages and our lives. They see us at our most vulnerable and use it against us. We must guard our hearts and minds against the Jodys and King Davids who would seek to take advantage of us. One advantage that we have as women today that Bathsheba did not is the ability to say no. Use it. Don't go when summoned. Run from temptation. Don't play the victim.

John and I made a rule pretty early on in his first deployment that, during his absence, men were not allowed in our house without their

---

1   "Your baby was lonely, as lonely could be / 'Til Jody provided the company. Ain't it great to have a pal / Who works so hard just to keep up morale"—a well-known military cadence.

wives. This wasn't put in place because my husband distrusts me but rather as a measure for my safety and the safety of our marriage. It guards us against unnecessary rumors that neighbors may start, and it protects me from being put in a frightening situation or in the line of temptation. In 1 John 2:15–17 (NET) we read, "Do not love the world or the things in the world. If anyone loves the world, the love of the Father is not in him, because all that is in the world (the desire of the flesh and the desire of the eyes and the arrogance produced by material possessions) is not from the Father but is from the world. And the world is passing away with all its desires, but the person who does the will of God remains forever." We are to flee temptation. That doesn't mean wait till it is upon you to run from it. Run before it ever reaches your door.

Esther had an advantage that Bathsheba did not. She was surrounded by women and eunuchs. There was no threat to her purity as she waited for her king. She was surrounded in a safe, protective environment. We need to surround ourselves in the same. Rumors are deadly to marriages when the spouse is across an ocean. No matter how much you trust your spouse, hearing a rumor of infidelity is debilitating. By giving no appearance of evil whatsoever, we are protecting our spouses' minds and hearts. By giving no reason for gossip, we become more valuable than jewels.

The heart of her husband trusts in her,

And he will have no lack of gain.

She does him good and not evil

All the days of her life.

~ Proverbs 31:11–12 NASB

DISCUSSION QUESTIONS

1. In your own words, describe loneliness.

2. What do you miss about your spouse more than anything? Share your thoughts.

3. In Genesis 4:7b (NET) God said to Cain, "sin is crouching at the door. It desires to dominate you, but you must subdue it." What was meant by this? How can sin dominate you, and what must you do to subdue it?

4. Do you have safeguards in place to protect your integrity and your spouse's heart?

5. Read Proverbs 31. What are some of the ways you can bring honor to your spouse? Do your actions here at home affect your spouse's career? How so?

CHAPTER 4

It's Not Always About Me

WHEN I FIRST APPROACHED THE idea of deployment, I did so selfishly. It did not dawn on me till D day the effect it would have on others in the family. Of course, I knew the children would miss their daddy, but they were so young. And his parents and mine, well, they rarely saw him as it was. So, selfishly, I went into deployment believing that as long as I knew what was going on, everything would be fine.

Esther did not keep her cousin Mordecai in the dark, and neither did Mordecai hide information from her. Upon hearing of Haman's plans to destroy the Jews, Mordecai expressed extreme grief. Esther 4:1 states that he tore his clothing and put on sackcloth and ashes. He was in no way silent as he walked through the city crying out with a bitter voice. He was so vocal in his grief that word traveled quickly to Esther. Despite her efforts to send clean clothing and mask his pain, he continued.

Early on in the book of Esther (2:20), we learn that Esther did whatever Mordecai asked of her, just as she had done while in his custody. Before she was taken from his home, before she was placed in the harem and given the title of queen, Esther respected Mordecai and followed his instructions. This is further displayed in her obedience to keep her heritage as a Jew secret on his instruction (2:10). When Esther sends her eunuch to question his behavior, Mordecai holds nothing back. He tells her in detail what has happened, what will happen, and how she must act.

With the respect that is due a queen and the firm love that is given a child, Mordecai calls on Esther to stand up and be strong in a way that only she can. Mordecai acknowledges her position as queen and as a Jew while confirming her appointed destiny to deliver her people. "It may very well be that you have achieved royal status for such a time as this!" That was a call to not wait idly by, hoping for safety, but rather to stand up and fulfill the appointing on her life and thereby directly impacting (in this case, physically saving) all of those around her.

It is at this point, with the validation of her cousin's words, that we see Esther act like a queen. With specific instructions for Mordecai to assemble the Jews and fast on her behalf, she prepares to go before the king, even though it may mean her life. It is at this point that Mordecai, the one who has been the instructor, faithfully follows instructions. Verse 4:17 says "So Mordecai set out to do everything that Esther had instructed him" (NET).

Even in the most difficult times, God is at work in the lives of those who love Him and remain faithful to Him.

Like Esther, there is another book of the Bible uniquely named after the heroine in its pages. In the book of Ruth, we are given a beautiful display of love between a widow and her mother-in-law. Destitute and broken, Naomi, who has lost her husband and two sons, decides to return home and urges her daughters-in-law to return to their own families. But Ruth refuses. She loves Naomi and commits to go where she goes, to worship her God, and to live with her mother-in-law (Ruth 1:16–17). Her words are endearing and used today in many marriage ceremonies because they are words of lifelong commitment and love.

Ruth held fast to her commitment to Naomi. She followed her instructions carefully, as she was in a foreign land that she wished to claim as her own. Ruth had no bearings regarding the culture of the people she now lived with. She relied heavily on Naomi's advice, and Naomi relied heavily on Ruth's trustworthiness and willingness to follow instructions. Because of the relationship these two women shared, because of Ruth's willingness to listen and heed Naomi's advice, and because of Naomi's great love for Ruth, God blessed them both with family. Ruth would later be included in the genealogy of King David and Jesus Christ.

Ruth and Esther were ordinary people who did what was necessary when it mattered most, sacrificed their own well-being, and were used by God in mighty ways because of it. What strikes me the most about their relationship with family during very difficult times is not how they acted; it is the character of the women that is displayed through their behavior leading up to the crisis. Both of these women had strong relationships with their family members. These relational ties, before the crisis occurred, greatly set the course for their behavior and actions once action became necessary.

We do not all come from picture perfect families. In fact, if I were to guess, perhaps none of us do. But neither did Esther or Ruth. Esther was an orphan raised by her cousin. Ruth was a widow faithfully dedicated to be the caregiver to her widowed mother-in-law. It is the steps we take prior to the crisis that allows us to remain strong and to be there for one another when the crisis occurs. Our relationships with immediate and extended family must be cultivated, nurtured, and respected prior to the first day of deployment. Having a basis of trust and respect makes communication so much easier during the difficult times. It is easier to explain to a loved one over the phone that you are not allowed to talk about certain dates or details if you have established a relationship built on trust and mutual respect. If that foundation is missing, then you may be accused of withholding information out of spite. It is important to remember that you are not the only one who is anxious for your spouse's well-being. Every friend and family member is traveling this journey with you.

First Corinthians 13, like Ruth 1:16–17, is used in the commitment ceremony of many weddings. Just as Ruth's vow of commitment, 1 Corinthians 13 was not originally penned for couples. Rather, 1 Corinthians 13 was written to the Corinthian church and was testament on how they should live every day. It is a model of how we should approach those in our lives that are both easy to love, and those who are difficult.

When Christ hung on the cross, He did not specify conditions but instead said, "Father, forgive them; they know not what they do" (Luke 23:34a KJV). He did not say *that one there, casting lots over my clothing, not him; he is being insensitive. Oh, and that one over there who whipped me, well, he caused me physical harm; let's not show him love and mercy. Yes, and that one, well, he is a threat to my disciples; let's just forget about him too.* No! Christ said, "FORGIVE THEM," and He was very clearly referring to the ones who were responsible for His death on the cross.

As a fellow military spouse, one who has endured the lonely nights and the fearful nightmares, I tell you that you are not alone. You are not the only one who loves your soldier. Look to his family and yours. Reach out to them. Not as one who holds all the cards but as one walking this journey alongside them. Your courage, your determination, your compassion to them in your own time of difficulty will be an example of love to them. Do not let pride rule your heart. As 1 Peter 5:6–7 (NASB) says, "Therefore humble yourselves under the mighty hand of God, that He may exalt you at the proper time, casting all your anxiety on Him because he cares for you." God can work amazing miracles with a humble heart open to His guidance.

DISCUSSION QUESTIONS

1. Prior to deployment, what type of relationship did you have with your extended family?

2. Would you say it changed during deployment? How so?

3. Read 1 Peter 5:8. Where else have we heard a similar verse?

4. Now keep reading. Write out 1 Peter 5:9–11 below and then circle God's promises found in these verses. How can they bring you comfort?

PART 3

Forced to Talk

CHAPTER 5

Forced to Talk

SOCRATES SAID, "A LIFE WHICH is unexamined is not worth living." I would add a marriage without examination is doomed. I learned a lot about my husband during his first deployment. So often when he is home, his voice gets drowned out by children, chores, and just the business of daily life. While he was gone, when Skype chimed, all that other clutter fell away and my attention went to my computer screen.

When I asked my husband what he thought of our year of talking, he so wisely quoted the Muppets nonsense song, "Mahna Mahna." Now, in all seriousness, he may have a point. Communication is difficult, and when you take away all the nonverbal clues that come with a conversation, sometimes meanings can be completely lost. (It's one of the reasons I prefer Skype over phone calls though, admittedly, looking into his face that I can't touch can be beyond excruciating at times.) There were conversations that, though I had waited hours and sometimes days to have, once I heard his voice, I might as well have been hearing only "mahna mahna." It was hard to listen with children calling out for attention or needing to run out the door to get to an appointment I'd already rescheduled twice. It was hard to listen to a pixelated face when all I wanted was a hand to hold.

Day 4 in *The Love Dare* is about thoughtfulness. "When you first fell in love, being thoughtful came quite naturally. You spent hours dreaming of what your loved one looked like, wondering what he or she was doing, rehearsing impressive things to say, then enjoying sweet memories of the time you spent together" (Kendrick 2009, 16). I would say that one benefit of deployment is that it brought me back to that stage. I will spend hours thinking through what to say, how to connect, but the struggle is actually connecting and expressing my love via cable lines. One thing I have learned is not to imply, hint, or assume John understands what I am saying. Chances are, if I don't say it clearly, he isn't going to catch it. That simple step has broken down so many barriers and allowed us to be honest about our dreams and daily expectations.

One thing we both had to remove from our dialogue was complaining. Not to say either of us has never fallen back into it, since it is a daily struggle to make sure the words from my mouth are pleasing to God. When all I get are snippets of conversations with my husband, and we are both miserable with not being together, the last thing either of us needs is to encumber each other further with complaint.

"She brings him good and not evil all the days of her life" (Proverbs 31:12 NET). Every disagreement we had during deployment stemmed around our perception of the event. While John was surrounded by fellow soldiers who risked their lives daily and were enveloped in a testosterone-adrenaline bubble, I was surrounded by children and spouses struggling through fear for their soldier and loneliness. Though we were both in deserts, our worldviews and those speaking into them were drastically different.

Stuart Diamond, Professor of Negotiation at Wharton Business School, writes in his book, *Getting More,* four questions to ask yourself when you are faced with a conflict: (a) What am I perceiving? (b) What are they perceiving? (c) Is there a mismatch? (d) If so, why? (Diamond 2012, 62). When we argue, it is not the time to compare one's life with the other. As John shared the sleepless long duty days and nights, he was not asking for me to compare my sleepless nights of crying children. When I did, it only confirmed his fear that I was not able to cope without him or maintain our home without his presence. While he needs to feel that we desire his presence, he also must have only the mission on his mind for his own safety and the safety of his fellow soldiers.

The Apostle Paul gives us advice on the words that proceed from our mouths, advice we should hold fast to in our marriages. Ephesians 4:29–32 (ESV) was written as instructions to the early church on how to create unity within church relationships. The same can be applied to our marriages.

> "Let no corrupting talk come out of your mouths, but only such as is good for building up, as fits the occasion, that it may give grace to those who hear. And do not grieve the Holy Spirit of God, by whom you were sealed for the day of redemption. Let all bitterness and wrath and anger and clamor and slander be put away from you, along with all malice. Be kind to one another, tenderhearted, forgiving one another, as God in Christ forgave you."

What do these verses look like across an ocean?

Corrupting talk is gossip and slander. It does not build up but tears down. My husband and I sometimes call this pillow talk. We confide in one another secrets that perhaps shouldn't be shared. These secrets are not ours to tell and place a burden of confidence on our spouse that they never agreed to. Sharing knowledge of affairs or failures of spouses back home just feeds the insecurities there and places a burden of secrecy between your spouse and a fellow soldier. Instead, share how a fellow military spouse was there for you, watched the kids, offered a kind word, or spent time with you. This builds up your friend, provides comfort to your spouse knowing you are not alone, and gives him something positive to share with his fellow soldier. What soldier wouldn't want to hear good news about their spouse an ocean away?

In verse 29, Paul is echoing Christ's words from Matthew 15:11 (NET): "What defiles a person is not what goes into the mouth; it is what comes out of the mouth that defiles a person." Words that are corrupting, unwholesome, rotten, and unprofitable harm the speaker and the one spoken about or to equally. When we use our words to tear down our husbands and make them feel useless, we are doing severe damage to our marriages and ourselves. Rather, we should use our words to build them up, to give them value, and to offer grace. Every individual word that comes from our mouths (whether in his presence or not) should be used to build our marriages, not destroy them.

When we use our words to destroy rather than to build up, verse 30 says we bring sorrow to the Holy Spirit. God grieves when we use words of destruction in our marriages, in our homes, and amongst our brothers and sisters in Christ. It is a powerfully frightening thought to know that my one offhand, lacking-grace comment causes the Holy Spirit to grieve. But why wouldn't it? If God truly loves each and every one of us as Scripture claims, then when one of us is injured, it hurts. If you are struggling with giving grace to your husband, I challenge you to stop looking at him as a man who has been put on this earth to bring you joy and instead begin to look at him as a child of God, a fellow brother in Christ, and a means by which you can bring God joy.

If you are unsure of how to give your husband grace in your words, of how to build him up rather than tear him down, verses 31–32 give a list of do's and don'ts. First, we are to put away bitterness, wrath, anger, clamor, slander, and malice. These have no room in a relationship of any kind. It is easy to get wrapped up in bitterness thinking of the days/months/years/birthdays/anniversaries (I really don't need to make a list; I'm sure you have one of your own) that your husband has missed because of the demands of his career. It is easy to hold on to past words or actions that in our minds wallow and drown out the kindness that has been shown us. These are not attributes that bring joy to life or to those around us. Clamor and slander are abusive, and shouting has no place in a marriage. Do not bring it into yours. Rather than an attitude of bitterness, a disposition toward anger and wrath, and the use of abusive speech, we should instead with all grace "Be kind to one another, tenderhearted, forgiving one another, as God in Christ forgave you" (v. 32 ESV).

Our attitude should be one of kindness, with a tenderhearted disposition and words of comfort and forgiveness. Just as we "have experienced the Lord's kindness" (1 Peter 2:3 NET), we should put away "all evil and all deceit and hypocrisy and envy and all slander" (2:1b NET). When we communicate with our husbands, whether it is for five minutes once a week or all day long, we should strive to speak words with kindness, not holding on to anything in the past that may weigh us down with bitterness. We should seek to create a better present and future full of tenderhearted intimacy.

Forgiveness must be quick in five-minute snippets of conversations. Both sides must seek words of kindness, be tender toward the needs of the other, and offer forgiveness when their own needs are not met. While John was in Iraq, he sent me a pair of pajamas, a cute skimpy shorts-and-top set. When he called via Skype and asked if I had received them, my response was yes, I love them. To which he replied, "Oh good, I was hoping they'd look half as good on you as the model." I smiled, said my I love yous, and logged off. Then I got the giggles. I chose to allow my husband's mistake to go uncorrected (for a time). I reminded myself of the testosterone bubble he was currently living in. Trust me, when he got back home, I reminded him of his words, and he apologized profusely. But the thing is I was never angry. In the past, I would have let a little slip up of that nature wreck my security. By consciously choosing not to harbor grudges, to try to view his comments in light of where he was rather than in my own insecurities, I was able to offer grace and forgiveness. It's a silly example, but I could have let it eat at me and slowly erode into bitterness and fear. Instead, it became a moment of lightheartedness. It brought laughter instead of anger.

Colossians 3:12b–14a (NET) tells how we are to love one another. We are to clothe ourselves "with a heart of mercy, kindness, humility, gentleness, and patience, bearing with one another and forgiving one another . . . and to all those virtues add love." It is important to incorporate each of these into our communication here at home and over long distances. Isaiah 42:20b (NLT) says, "You hear with your ears, but don't really listen." When we are so ready to give a reply, seek out an offense, or justify our own words, we fail to hear what our partner is trying to say. I must give up my need to be right or to cast judgement;

I must listen even harder when I hear something that I do not understand. I must put into context (his context not mine) what is being said. And I must give grace, forgive the blunders, and love.

Deployment is lonely, plain and simple. I think that word sums it up more than any other. Many times I have felt like the psalmist who wrote, "Look right, look left—there's not a soul who cares what happens! I'm up against it, with no exit—bereft, left alone" (Psalm 142:4 MSG).

Anne Bradstreet wrote in the poem to her husband, "Still wait with doubts, and hopes, and failing eye, / His voice to hear or person to descry" (Bradstreet 1897, 273). In 1678 the separation of an ocean with letters that traveled slowly, back and forth by ship, was painful. While Bradstreet's circumstances are foreign to us, the pain of separation is not.

But we are not alone. Isaiah 58:11a (NASB) says, "The Lord will continually guide you, and satisfy your desire." Throughout the book of Esther, God's name is never used. He never interjects instructions or encouragement, and yet it is obvious that He intervenes on Esther's behalf. Esther was not alone. She had the love of Mordecai and the favor of all who saw her. She sought the counsel of others God had put in her path, and she listened. At times it seems that we are also alone, left to work out the difficulties of parenthood and deployments alone. But we are not; we have one another, fellow military spouses who are enduring the same hardships. Some have already done this more than once and would be more than happy to share their learned wisdom with newer spouses. There is joy to be found in helping one another.

DISCUSSION QUESTIONS

1. Prior to deployment, what did you and your spouse spend the majority of your time doing? Did you talk? About what?

2. If your soldier is currently deployed, how would you say your conversations have changed?

3. What is something you would like to be able to talk about with your spouse but do not feel you can over Skype/FaceTime/e-mail? Why? Take a few moments and think of ways you can bring it up.

CHAPTER 6

Facing Our Father

BEFORE SETTING OUT TO PETITION King Xerxes, Esther called on all of the Jews in Susa to fast for three days, and she and her female attendants did the same (4:16). Before going before the king with a request that could have cost her life, she approached the King of the universe, who held her destiny in His hands. She did not seek Him alone. She asked her community to join her.

Psalm 31 speaks words of comfort. Though my enemies are not the same as those of the author of this psalm, they are real. My enemies are fear, loneliness, depression, and doubt. They surround me on all sides, robbing me of joy and sleep.

> In you, O Lord, I have taken shelter!
> Never let me be humiliated!
> Vindicate me by rescuing me!
> Listen to me!
> Quickly deliver me!
> Be my protector and refuge,
> a stronghold where I can be safe!
>
> ~ Psalm 31:1–2 NET

The psalmist uses the words *shelter, protector, refuge, stronghold,* and *safe* throughout Psalm 31. We can seek shelter in the arms of Christ! What a beautiful, comforting thought that instead of being overcome by the insomnia of loneliness and the depression that fear brings, I can rest safely in the shelter of my protector!

But I trust in the Lord

I will be happy and rejoice in your faithfulness,

because you notice my pain

and you are aware of how distressed I am.

~ Psalm 31:6b–7 NET

Though we at times feel alone and utterly abandoned, as if no one can understand, the Lord is trustworthy. Dwell on that. He does not leave! Though we may feel He is not listening, He is. Listen to the psalmist's words in verse 22: "I jumped to conclusions and said, 'I am cut off from your presence!' But you heard my plea for mercy when I cried out to you for help."

He hears us! Do you hear that? Let it sink in. The God of this universe hears us. He knows before we even tell Him that we worry for our soldier's safe return, that we are pained by the look in our children's eyes or the sobs we hear from their bedrooms. He knows our distress and despair. He hears us! And more than that, He enables us to endure! Though we may be in a place where no one understands what we are going through, He does. We can be utterly friendless, completely cut off from the military community and family and our soldier, and yet we are not alone. We can rest safely in God's hands, knowing it is He who controls are destiny.

Psalm 31 speaks to the distress of the psalmist and the comfort and trustworthiness of God. We can cry out to God in our moments of weakness. When the tears come and the ache of distance overwhelms us, when no one seems to understand and they shy away from our puffy eyes and brokenness, we can still trust in God. He will not leave us. He will comfort us.

> But I trust in you, O Lord!
> I declare, "You are my God!"
> You determine my destiny!
>
> ~ Psalm 31:14–15a NET

I love Psalm 31:16: "Smile on your servant! Deliver me because of your faithfulness!" The God of this universe, smile on me! Bring me to a place where my life reflects Your glory. May His love, friendship, and favor shine so brightly in each of our lives that He is all others see when we pass them.

A friend recently lost her husband. As we offered her hugs and "so sorry for your loss" statements, she comforted us instead. With unfailing trust in God, she declared, "You are my God, You control my destiny." She spoke of the peace with which God had comforted her. She spoke of joy in the midst of this trial. Then, when we thought we had shed every tear we could for her, she began to sing "Blessed be Your Name." I was forever changed. I was forever comforted. Her life reflected His glory. For a moment in time, she shared with me and every other woman there what joy in Christ means. May we always find praise in our hearts no matter the suffering, no matter how much pain there is in the offering. Only Christ can offer that peace in the midst of life's most painful moments.

Be strong and confident! The Lord is your strength! No matter where you are, remember this: you were not called "for such a time as this" to walk alone. The Lord will guide you, strengthen you, and walk with you. Seek Him in prayer, tell Him your struggles and your desires, and praise Him for the refuge He provides you.

The Lord offers so much to us. More than just refuge. In 1 Peter 5:8 (NET) we read, "Be sober and alert. Your enemy the devil, like a roaring lion, is on the prowl looking for someone to devour." Satan is looking for the opportunity to hinder our fellowship with the Lord and to destroy our testimony. Colossians 2:8 (NET) warns us to "be careful not to allow anyone to captivate you through an empty, deceitful philosophy that is according to human traditions and the elemental spirits of the world, and not according to Christ." It is easy to get caught up in the quick fixes of the world to ease our loneliness. But how much more satisfying it is in the long term to seek the support of our Lord through prayer. The momentary good feelings that the world offers us are just that, momentary. They do not bring strength to our relationships with the Lord or with our soldier. "We are not ignorant of 'Satan's' schemes" (2 Corinthians 2:11b), but rather, knowing full well that he seeks to destroy us, we MUST seek shelter in the Lord's presence. In the Lord's stronghold. In the Lord's safe protecting hands.

Prayer is the key to seeking refuge in Christ. It is the key to resisting temptation. The Lord already defeated sin on the cross! Who better to rely on than the One who has already won? Satan is nothing more than an ankle biter who has no real power over Christ. Sin is irrational in the presence of the grace of God.

If we do not believe that we are sinners, that sin separates us from the perfect God, that Jesus Christ came, died, and rose again for our sins so that we can be in fellowship with God for all eternity, then prayer is pointless. "Now without faith it is impossible to please him, for the one who approaches God must believe that he exists and that he rewards those who seek him" (Hebrews 11:6 NET). If you do not believe, seek Him and ask that He give you the necessary faith to believe. Because without that faith, we cannot receive the strength that comes from a relationship with Him.

There is no need to be defeated, down, distressed, or discouraged in your daily living when you realize that the Savior will work out all the details of your life if you leave them with Him. It is in Christ that we have complete victory. Rest in the promises found in Romans 8:37 and 1 Corinthians 15:57. There is no reason to fear, "because the one who is in you is greater than the one who is in the world" (1 John 4:4b NET). Jesus Christ, who lives in you, with whom you seek fellowship through prayer, is greater than sin or any temptation you face.

There are times that perhaps I caught a snippet of news coverage or we went as a unit into communication silence until all family members of a fallen soldier are contacted. During that time, I cannot breathe as I anticipate a knock on the door. In these moments, I do not always know what to call out to God. I seek my husband's safety but also that of his friends and their families. My heart breaks. Romans 8:26 (NET) says, "In the same way, the Spirit helps us in our weakness, for we do not know how we should pray, but the Spirit himself intercedes for us with inexpressible groanings." I seek His comfort during those times that words fail me. He understands fully what I need.

"Therefore let us confidently approach the throne of grace to receive mercy and find grace whenever we need help" (Hebrews 4:16
NET). We have access to the ear of the God of this universe. He lis-
tens. Even when we don't know the words to speak. He understands.
He protects. And He provides comfort.

DISCUSSION QUESTIONS

1. Take a few moments to think about your prayer life. Not quantity but quality. Are you honest with God about your fears and your feelings?

2. Do you turn to God in your fear? Do you allow Him to comfort you?

3. There have been a number of songs throughout my journey that have ministered to me. Is there one song in particular that helps you? If so, why?

4. What about a verse? Do you have a particular verse you hold tightly to right now in your life? Why that one?

PART 4

Why Me? Why This?

CHAPTER 7

Why Me? Why This?

I CRIED,

>Lord, I'm so afraid tonight.
>There's no rest for my soul.
>Besieged by worry, fear, and pain,
>I tossed and turned and rolled.

I prayed,

>Lord, send your angel,
>Someone to hold my hand,
>Someone to touch my broken heart
>And say, "I understand."

I prayed,

>Lord, send a candle
>To light this long, dark night,
>A flame to warm and cheer me,
>To set my soul aright.

I prayed,

>Lord, send . . .

Then, that was all.

For what He sent to me

Was peace.

His everlasting arms

Carried me off

To sleep.

~ By Ann Luna (Clairmont 1999, 127)

Perhaps it is because we are located in the desert of Fort Bliss. Perhaps it is simply a time that God is using to teach me to trust Him even when I do not always feel His presence. Whatever the reason, I have found God speaking to me through the stories of wanderings through the desert.

The Israelites were removed from the fertile soil of the Nile (also a land of enslavement filled with idolatry) and were en route to the Promised Land. God kept them turning in circles in the desert for forty years in order to prepare them for the blessings He wished to give them, the blessings He had promised them. In the in-between, the Israelites developed a complaining spirit. Author Jeff Manion calls this "The Land Between." He writes, "The heart drifts toward complaint as if by gravitational pull—after all, complaint seems a reasonable response to a sequence of disappointing events. Generally, you don't have to extend an invitation for complaint to show up. It arrives as an uninvited guest" (Manion 2010, 55).

Complaint is all around me in the desert of El Paso. I hear it at FRG meetings, lines in Walmart, frustrations over the language barriers, about the schools, lack of housing, wind, dust, heat—the list is never-ending. Complaint is in my own heart as well: the long lonely nights, too many fundraisers, too many marriages crumbling around me, the drama of single parenting while being pulled in too many directions by too many commitments and the familiar ring of Skype at the worst possible moment when, more than anything, you want to talk to and hold your soldier, but you don't want him to see the piles of laundry behind you or the applesauce lathered into your hair.

In one sense, Esther's world is not one I live in: eunuchs, royalty, golden goblets, luxurious couches, banquets, perfumed baths, and a beauty contest for one man's heart.

In another sense, it is: waiting for loved ones to return from war, loneliness, longing, surrounded by women living through the same struggle, the quietness of God, the realization that God has orchestrated my placement "for such a time as this."

Esther was an orphaned Jew forced into captivity and a beauty contest in the hope of becoming a bride. I was neither forced nor competed for my position. I chose this life. I chose my husband, and he chose me. I hear over and over, "My husband enlisted in the Army. I didn't sign up for this." Esther truly could say those words; she never signed up to be an orphan or to be a participant in a beauty contest where the prize was a man shared with an entire harem. And yet, she never complains.

We live in a world of instant gratification. A world that flies in the face of what we, as military spouses, are called to do. We are called to WAIT. Waiting can be painful, but it is also rewarding. It strengthens and matures us. It is not only our spouse we are waiting on; it is an understanding of God's purpose for us through this time. Many times that purpose will not reveal itself to us, perhaps not even in this lifetime. "God can seem too distant, too slow in appearing, too unaccommodating to individual desires. The consequent longings easily seduce into adulterous liaisons with more immediately satisfying gods." So instead we chase after meaningless things, fill our days with friends of the opposite sex, lengthy Facebook chats, or activities we know our spouse and our Savior would not approve of. "But when the afternoon's diversion has passed, unfulfillment comes raging back with even greater intensity. By then, though, the marriage has been defiled, the God of salvation has been betrayed" (McCullough 1995, 15).

There was a time in my life where I struggled with the goodness of God. I did not trust or rely solely on Him. I often find myself drifting back there in my mind, my faith, and my attitude. When my daughter was diagnosed with cancer at only six months of age, I became very angry and bitter. I turned away from the God I knew could heal my baby but chose not to. I have never prayed so hard in my life. I knew in my heart that God had already healed her. I thanked Him for the healing. I believed.

I've walked this Christian life long enough to know that things do not always turn out the way we ask, but I had also experienced, witnessed firsthand, miracles occur. I knew that my God was strong enough to heal my daughter. And since He claimed to love her more than I ever could, I knew that at any moment one of the doctors would walk into the waiting room and say, "We can't explain it, but there is no tumor. Your daughter can keep her eye. The cancer is gone."

That was not the path that had been laid out for us. Instead, when they walked in the room, what was said was, "Everything went according to plan. The surgery went well. You can go see her in recovery now." The room spun.

What I did not see at that time was the healing that did take place. I was so consumed in my grief I did not see God's hand in every step: the willingness of the eye doctor to see us within 24 hours of calling, the quick response of the specialist or the fact that he had only just attended a retinoblastoma seminar with our daughter's future doctors, the kindness of both of our employers in giving us as much time as we needed off, the blessing of a hospital that took care of every detail, and the support system of fellow St. Jude parents that came with the package.

Our daughter's life was saved, just not in the way I had requested.

The next few weeks were emotional, to say the least. People do not know how to respond to tragedy. I am one of them. I have stumbled many times attempting to find words to offer comfort.

Our first time out, after the enucleation, I took her to Chick-fil-A, and another parent began to berate me for bringing my child out in public with pink eye. "Um, ma'am, look a little closer. She doesn't have an eye." Or the time a man walked around a corner and exclaimed, "Oh my! A pirate baby!" Or the first church service after her surgery where the subject of faith was preached on: "If you just have enough faith, healing will come!" No . . . it didn't.

I entered a very dark place. I was angry and hurt. I had a misconstrued image of God.

After being a Christian for over twenty years, four years of seminary, overseas mission trips, and working in ministry, one would think that when tragedy hit my own life, I would be able to hold fast to my faith. No. I let go.

I now see God's hand in every person He placed in my life during that time. Strangers I met in waiting rooms offered to pray for me. Into my life came new friends whose struggle with cancer was much greater but who constantly held on to joy and belief in God's goodness. Old friends would remind me that I wasn't being asked to carry tomorrow, only today.

God never let me go, though I wanted nothing to do with Him.

All I could see was that He had the power to heal my daughter and had turned His back. Thankfully, God did not give up on me.

Life had found a new normal. But I was empty.

It was not until we arrived at Fort Bliss that I began to see how God had intricately woven Himself into my life and had not allowed me to slip away.

I joined PWOC (Protestant Women of the Chapel) in the hope of finding friends. It worked. I soon joined a class based on Phillip Yancey's book *The Jesus I Never Knew* and dove into Bible study and a fresh look at Christ. At that time, I hadn't picked up my Bible in a year. As someone who had committed her life to work in full-time ministry, I was in the midst of a crisis of identity as well as a crisis of faith.

And then something happened.

Christ spoke to me through the story of Lazarus.

The story of Lazarus is found in John 11, but it was verse 21 that jumped out at me.

> Martha said to Jesus, "Lord, if you had been here, my brother would not have died" (NET)

When Jesus first heard of Lazarus being sick, Scripture says He loved Lazarus and his sister, and He waited. In my world, and I am sure in Martha's as well, *He waited* does not communicate love.

Jesus did not arrive until four days after Lazarus died. Martha was the first to greet Him and the first to ask "Where were you?" Jesus did not rebuke her. Instead, He listened. In verse 35, He wept.

Suddenly the flood gates opened, and for the first time I mourned my daughter's loss, I mourned her sight, I mourned the direction our life had turned, and I cried out to God, "WHERE WERE YOU?"

And I felt His comfort.

Jesus loved Lazarus, Martha, and Mary. He grieved with them. He hurt because they hurt, even though He knew the miracle He was about to perform. The coming resurrection of Lazarus could not bring comfort to his sisters yet because they could not understand it. Their pain was real, and Jesus hurt with them. With them. With me.

For the first time I began to realize that my daughter was healed; maybe not in the way I asked, but that did not negate the fact that she was healthy. I had misconstrued His allowing pain in her life and ours as if He was saying He did not love my baby. Nothing could be farther from the truth.

There are moments along the journey that become too heavy to bear. Throughout Scripture we hear people crying out to God that they want this burden removed from them. Yet, instead of allowing each of them to remain in despair, God reaches out to them and gives them the strength needed to continue.

Moses wanted nothing more to do with the Israelites and their complaining spirit. He would rather die. The Lord answered Moses by giving him men to help him lead and by answering the complaints of the Israelites and providing them with the food they requested (Numbers 11:14–23).

In 1 Kings 19:3–4, Elijah is running from Jezebel and lets the Lord know he wishes to die. Rather than grant his request, the Lord comforts Elijah in his despair by providing him with food, drink, and rest. When that was not enough, the Lord met with him, reaffirmed his calling, and provided him with a companion (19:5–16).

Lazarus' death and resurrection isn't the only time in the Bible that Christ chose not to act. In Matthew 26:36-46, Jesus in the Garden of Gethsemane asked that the cup be taken from Him. And God's answer was no.

Christ wept and cried out to God, "Let this cup pass from me" (Matthew 26:39b NET). He felt forsaken, but He also said, "Yet not what I will, but what you will" (Matthew 26:39c). Yancey writes, "At its core Gethsemane depicts, after all, the story of an unanswered prayer. The cup of suffering was not removed" (Yancey 2002, 195). The whole reason Christ came to earth was to bridge the gap between us and God. The cross was His purpose, but it was a purpose of suffering. The cross was necessary for our salvation, though it caused much pain. The Lord knows of despair and loneliness. In the Garden of Gethsemane, when He was facing the time of His death, Jesus cried out to the Father to "let this cup pass from me." He sought the comfort of His companions, His disciples, and instead found them sleeping.

Christ could have insisted that this was not the way and ended the story right then and there. But He choose not to act, not to save Himself, but to submit to God's will. In doing so, a greater story was written. A story of our salvation.

Perhaps your story is similar to mine. Perhaps it is different in the details but similar in the pain. Know that Christ weeps with you. In the quietness of your room late at night when you pour out your heart, or in the crowded room where you wear your game face, He knows you are hurting and wants to walk through your suffering with you. "Blessed are those who mourn, for they will be comforted" (Matthew 5:4 NET).

Before John first deployed, I attended a pre-deployment conference. The speaker, Beatrice Fishback, author of *Loving Your Military Man*, compared deployment to cancer (a battle she was facing at that time). The rest of the lecture was lost on me as I began breathing exercises to halt the panic attack rising in my chest. I was still dealing with the cancer that claimed my daughter's eye and believed I was not in a position, spiritually or physically, to survive the trauma again, nor was my marriage.

With time I learned the truth of Beatrice Fishback's words. Deployment and cancer do have similarities. Both are outside of my control. Total trust must be placed on God, trust that He knows the outcome and knows what I can and cannot handle. There must be faith that God will not only provide the strength but the friendships to help when needed. Total reliance on God alone must be given because He is the only one who can heal, the only one who never forsakes, and the only one who can comfort us during the long, lonely nights. On the other side of cancer and on the other side of deployment, there is a newfound love for one's spouse and children, a new found strength, and a deeper sense of trust in God, who has proved faithful through the journey. It is a journey that once you reach the other side, you would not trade because of the person you have become.

Christ knew what it was like to be utterly alone. He does not ask more of us than He endured. And yet, He willingly said, knowing full well what lay ahead, "Yet not my will, but what you will" (Matthew 26:39c). I long for that faith. So many times I am more like Elijah, crying out to just let it end, that no one could possibly understand the loneliness and desperation. But just like He did for Moses, the Lord has given me companions for this journey. Just like He did for Elijah, God continuously places that one person who has also said goodbye to her husband and is in a season of waiting, alongside me. And just as He did for Christ, He asks that I walk this road so that His will be done. I do not have to understand what that is; I only have to trust.

DISCUSSION QUESTIONS

1. Have you ever been so angry and confused by unanswered prayers that you have walked away from your faith? What brought you back? Are you back?

2. Beatrice Fishback uses the illustration of cancer to describe deployment. Do you think this is a fair description? Why or why not?

3. Who else in Scripture cried out to God to have their burden removed? Did God answer them or leave them in their despair?

4. How have you been inspired by someone in your own life who demonstrated faith during tragedy or suffering?

CHAPTER 8

The Other Wife

"IF THE ARMY WANTS YOU to have a wife, then they will issue you one."

I've heard this joke more than once, and the more I hear it, the more it sounds like fact. The military is not kind to marriages. It's hard. I have seen this lifestyle break far more homes than I have seen it strengthen. As much as we would wish to be, the military spouse is not consistently the number one priority for a soldier—and cannot be. The soldier's mind has to be on the mission, especially during deployments.

In Genesis 16, we come across two women, Sarai and Hagar. Sarai is Abram's wife, and Hagar is her maidservant. When Sarai could not conceive children, she "issued" her husband a second wife, Hagar. Hagar appears to have instantly become pregnant and gained the contempt of Sarai. Suddenly, Abram's attention is diverted from Sarai to the new mother and child. Eventually, Sarai (now called Sarah) gives birth to a child. But in her jealousy toward Hagar, she drives a wedge between Abram (now called Abraham) and Hagar and demands that the woman and child be banished. And Abraham follows orders.

I have occasionally felt like Hagar, the other wife. My husband has no choice but to jump when called, despite what we might be in the middle of or the obligations of home. Deployment rips him from our home and drives a wedge between him, myself, and the children. But it is unavoidable.

What I love most about the story of Hagar is that God did not leave her abandoned in the wilderness. He met with her. He heard her.

The Lord spoke to Hagar and blessed her. He promised her and her son, Ishmael, life, and she named the Lord "You are a God of seeing." He looked down and saw her at her most desperate, and He did not forget her but looked after her and cared for her.

A God of Seeing! He sees us. When we feel overlooked and neglected, God still sees us! He hasn't forgotten us and will not abandon us in our hour of need. How comforting to know that we are loved!

Each one of God's names opens up a greater understanding, terror, and beauty of who God is. His names are aspects of Himself He has chosen to reveal to us, and they are demonstrations of who the authors of Scripture understood him to be. There is power in a name. There is beauty and fear. There is creation and destruction, destiny and love all wrapped up in one word.

We struggle as humans to see God. We often box Him in to our dim version of who we believe He should be. The power in a name is that it opens our minds to see more of who He is.

Names evoke feelings and memories. They give identity to an individual and a sense of belonging to a group. They bring forth both understanding and assumptions. As parents, we spend months selecting and crafting the perfect names for our children.

We run them through a gamut of possible nicknames, remembering fondly and with fear pet names bestowed on us. We search out meanings, hoping to shape the course of our child's life for good. We list our favorite literary characters and family members who have brought joy to our life until, finally, we find that one perfect name our child will carry for the rest of his or her life. That name is a reflection not only on the child but also on us, the parents, and all the hopes and anticipation we place on that new life.

As I grew up, my name was manipulated, shortened, and rhymed to provide entertainment for others. The P was purposely left out, or it was lengthened to rhyme with dopey, and it was added to verse to declare my love for smoking "dope with the pope on a rope." In middle school, I attempted to have others refer to me by my middle name, but *Hope* was just too easy to rhyme with and *Nadine* never caught on. Despite my short stint in middle school, I love my name. It has been a call on my life. When I have struggled through moments of depression, frustration, and lack of faith, it has reminded me of who I am. It has reminded me of my parents' joy and faith at my birth. There is power in a name.

It should come as no surprise that the study of God's names would bring us closer to an understanding of Him and those who have interacted with Him in Scripture. Sarah laughed in disbelief at her first God encounter. Hagar, the other wife, stood in awe of the God who sees. Hold that close. A God who sees. Hagar found Him in her desert, her abandonment, and her grief, and so can we.

Hagar wasn't the only *other* wife in Scripture.

Esther shared her king with an entire harem and all of Persia. Though he chose her as his queen, when it came time to tell him her heritage, she was nervous for he had not called for her in a month. The honeymoon was over, it seems; chances are that someone else was sharing his bed. When Mordecai told her she must go before the king to save her people, she was terrified for her own life. Persia, not Esther, was the king's first love. By approaching him, she was disobeying a Persian law; by telling him of the plot, she had to confess her omission of facts. She would be asking him to reverse an irreversible law, and she would be going up against his right-hand man. The king of Persia, who had not called for her company in a month, was about to be asked the impossible, and she was rightly terrified. Esther knew, partly from the example of his first queen's disposal, that Persia's needs outweighed her own life. In Esther 5 we read that she went before the king despite her fear. God had stationed her in this position in life. He had placed her in the king's inner circle "for such a time as this" (Esther 4:14b NET), and He would protect her as she followed this path.

Leah, though Jacob's first bride, came second to the love of his life, Rachel. The competition between these two sisters had repercussions in their children's interactions. Genesis 29:31a (ESV) states, "When the Lord saw that Leah was hated, he opened her womb." God saw Leah's loneliness and rejection as the other wife, and He blessed her. He did not allow her to go without her husband's favor. In fact, He blessed her with many sons. He did not allow her to be pushed to the side, forgotten, unwanted. Rachel saw Leah's blessing and became jealous, and suddenly a race for who could bless Jacob the most began. Each wife gave their servants to Jacob to bear more children. Competition reared its ugly head. The competition became so heated that the two women began to barter for time in Jacob's bed; at one point, Rachel sold her evening rights to the *other* wife for a handful of mandrakes, known for their fertility. Between the two women, their handmaids, and intense jealousy, Jacob was blessed with twelve sons and a daughter.

When we list our priorities in marriage seminars, marriage books, couple's Sunday school classes, and even in sermons, the list goes something like this: God, spouse, family, career. When soldiers list their priorities during deployments it more closely falls: mission, battle buddies, family. We often hear *family first,* but it's just not the case for those with military spouses. It can't be. Life isn't a constant. It can't be managed by a stagnant list of priorities, even if you are not a military family. There is an ebb and flow in our responsibilities, our passions, and our callings. When we are both on the same side of the planet, it makes sense to hold each other as a higher priority. When we are an ocean away, there are times when surviving is the only priority. I would much rather my husband come home to me than to have him thinking about me and making our relationship his #1 in the midst of enemy territory. As long as we are both committed to our marriage lasting, we can work on us later. Now when he is on Skype, I want his full attention, and he is deserving of mine.

Hagar discovered she was never alone. Though abandoned by the father of her son, God saw her and met her at the well. Esther, though fearful for her own life due to the king's loyalty to Persia, found courage to face the unknown and to stand in the gap for others. Leah and Rachel, rather than resting in God's blessings in their lives, began to compete for their man's attention. Instead of basking in the knowledge that the God of this universe sees us as Hagar did, instead of finding courage to stand up for such a time as this as Esther did, these sisters fell into misery. They allowed their situation and their desires to dictate their days and nights. Don't allow yourself to fall into the trap these sisters fell into. Instead, follow the example of Hagar and Esther. Know that you are loved and cherished by God. He sees you and even positions you where you are. He equips and encourages you along the way, offering comfort and courage if you will only accept it from Him. You are not unseen.

DISCUSSION QUESTIONS

1. Read Genesis 16:1–14. Have you ever felt utterly abandoned like Hagar, only to discover God has never left you? Share with the group.

2. Leah and Rachel competed for their husband's attention. Have you ever competed for your spouse's attention? Maybe competing with his career, hobby, or friend? Did you come out the winner?

CHAPTER 9

Bitterness and Self-Pity

IT WAS THE FIRST DAY of soldiers being reunited with their families in our church . . . all except mine. John's unit has been gone nine months, and most had returned home. According to the news, the Iraqi war was over, and all combat troops returned home. Um, wait a minute . . . where is my soldier? Iraq. Yes, the news was wrong. Surprised? Not really.

That day at church, I felt as if I was being looked at as a wounded puppy. Sometimes I think the projections we place on people are worse than what they are really thinking. In my mind, it went something like this: "Poor thing. I wish I could just shoot her and put her out of her misery." In reality, thoughts were along the lines of "I truly wish you could be as happy as I am right now."

James 1:2–4 (NASB) puts me in my place as I desperately want to complain, throw my hands up, and just scream "Why?" Scripture quietly answers back, "Consider it all joy, my brethren, when you encounter various trials, knowing that the testing of your faith produces endurance. And let endurance have its perfect result, so that you may be perfect and complete, lacking in nothing."

I know the feeling of a husband returning. It is sheer joy in my world. I don't resent other spouses at all for their experience. I am thrilled, even ecstatic for them when their soldiers come home, and eagerly anticipate my time. Joy is not something that happens to us; it is a decision we make. Yes, there is envy in my heart, but I will not let it draw me into bitterness or self-pity. God has a mission for me and my husband that is not yet complete.

What struck me that day was the image of Esther, quietly waiting in the harem for her turn with the king. She was not the first contestant in this beauty pageant, and perhaps not the last. She watched as, one by one, beautiful women walked into the bedchamber of her future husband. If she had allowed bitterness or self-pity to overtake her, would she have been as striking to the king when it was her turn? Would God still have been able to use her to turn the eyes of royalty and place her in such a prominent position?

When it was Esther's turn to go to the king, she "met with the approval of all who saw her" and "the king loved Esther more than all the other women, and she met with his loving approval more than all the other young women" (Esther 2:15b, 17a NET). Yes, Esther was beautiful, but even the most beautiful woman with a scowl on her face is unpleasant to be near. Proverbs 15:13 NET says, "A joyful heart makes the face cheerful, but by a painful heart the spirit is broken." I know that when I am tired and discouraged or feel unappreciated or that life just isn't fair, it shows on my face. The eyes always give us away.

Esther did not display a spirit of bitterness or complaint. We don't hear that she spent her time complaining to her eunuch of her capture, nor do we hear jealousy regarding the women who had already entered the king's chamber. What we read is that she "met with the approval of ALL who saw her." That includes the other young women in the harem. Had she been harboring resentment, these women with whom she spent her entire day every day would have noticed.

"Pursue peace with everyone, and holiness, for without it no one will see the Lord. See to it that no one comes short of the grace of God, that no one be like a bitter root springing up and causing trouble, and through him many become defiled" (Hebrews 12:14-15 NET). These verses speak into Esther's situation. Without her placement in the king's household, death would have come to the Jews. Esther's gentle spirit enabled her to save a nation. Our gentle spirit—and unwavering decision not to become bitter or full of self-pity—may just be the saving grace to our marriage.

My husband's job was not done; there was more for him still to do. Part of honoring John is not coming to him with a bitter spirit. To hear me complain of the unfairness of it all would only add to his pain at being separated from his family. Through my own acceptance of our situation and separation, we could both strive to seek the Lord's will in the details, rather than our own. Had either one of us turned into the "bitter root," it would have made the separation only more difficult.

Thinking of Esther growing up in Mordecai's household, I wonder if Esther was familiar with Job's story. Though it follows the book of Esther in placement, it occurred more than a thousand years before Esther found herself as queen. Job was no stranger to strife. His response to disaster was not unlike Esther's. It was one of acceptance. My one year of separation in no way compares to his great loss of children, livestock, possessions, and livelihood. Job's loss far outweighs my own, and through it I can learn some amazing lessons from his choice of faith and his words of pain. I can also learn a great deal from his wife's response.

Job was not shy about sharing his pain with God. Though he sat in silence with his friends for seven days, his pain was so great that when he did speak, he cursed the day of his birth. His suffering far outweighed any good he had previously experienced. His pain was intense. Well-meaning friends tried to offer comfort but could not even begin to understand what Job was going through. Job was alone in his grief. Except he wasn't. He had the God who sees watching and listening.

Sometimes, in the midst of our pain, we forget that God cares. It can feel very much like we are forgotten. When my six-month-old went back for surgery to have her cancer and eye removed, I prayed with every fiber of my being that the Lord would, just in the last minute, reach down and heal her and make the surgery unnecessary. He could have. I have friends He has done this for. So I believed with all my being He would do the same for my child. And when He didn't, I let bitterness win.

I chose at that time to focus on what was lost. I could not see what was gained or saved. My daughter's life was saved. All I saw was the no to my prayer. All I saw was the empty eye socket rather than the beating heart and the steady breath of my child. I allowed my anger, bitterness, and self-pity to win, and I walked away from the comfort of Christ.

"Yet you do not know what your life will be like tomorrow. You are just a vapor that appears for a little while and then vanishes away" (James 4:14 NASB).

In my journey through Scripture and through my Christian faith, I had missed an important lesson. I had heard the stories of believers who had willingly accepted God's will of suffering. I had read the patience of Job, the faith of Elijah, and the strength of the martyrs. I had prayed Christ's prayer in Gethsemane: "thy will be done" (Matthew 26:42b KJV). We are given these stories years, centuries, and millennia after they have occurred. They are held up as models of how we should respond in the face of tragedy. We gloss over the humanity, the fear, and the questions that are asked in those moments of trial.

Job questions God. "Therefore I will not restrain my mouth; I will speak in the anguish of my spirit, I will complain in the bitterness of my soul" (7:11 ESV). He curses the day he was born. His patience has ended, and he is ready for his life to end as well. Then God answers. He doesn't leave Job alone to wallow in self-pity. He reminds him that He, God, has created the monsters of this world and the beauty. There is a purpose behind Job's suffering, though Job is not privy to the reason.

Elijah, overcome with fear and exhaustion, asked the Lord to take his life. He was done, exhausted and weary of a life of persecution (1 Kings 19). God did not leave him to die. He fed him and encouraged him. God had a plan, and Elijah was part of it.

Martha went out to Jesus as He came to her. Lazarus had been four days in the grave. She had called for Him when Lazarus was sick. She had been witness to His miracles of healing the sick and giving sight to the blind. Martha, Mary, and Lazarus were His friends. He loved them. Martha called, and Jesus did not answer. "Lord, if you had been here, my brother would not have died" (John 11:21b NET).

There is no question; she knows because she has seen. But God had a plan bigger than His love for one family.

Soon it would be Jesus' turn. He would weep alone in the Garden of Gethsemane. Matthew 26:38 says that his soul was grieved to the point of death. First Job, then Elijah, and now Jesus have found the pain unbearable. All three approach God with their grief. What stands out in Jesus' prayer is not a question of God's plan but an acknowledgement of not wanting to endure the suffering, yet being willing to go forward with the knowledge that it is necessary. Jesus wept and sweat blood over the anticipation of the pain that He would experience, and yet He still said, "My Father, if this cup cannot be taken away unless I drink it, your will must be done" (Matthew 26:42b NET). Though His Son asked to be spared, God sent Him to the cross. God had a plan bigger than His love for His Son.

It is okay to ask questions. The answers come only when the questions are asked. Curiosity about God and His plan for our lives draws us to Him. It leads us to Scripture and prayer.

I silenced the questions after my daughter's surgery. I no longer wanted to hear what God had in store for any of us. Thankfully, as with Elijah, God did not let me go in defeat. He waited patiently for me to find my way back to Him, and along the way He shaped and strengthened my faith without me even knowing what was happening. He continued to place people and situations in my life that would ultimately draw me back to Him. I let bitterness win, but God wasn't going to let it defeat me. He had a plan for my family and for me.

Throughout that first deployment, I kept a devotional beside my bed, *Faith Deployed* by Jocelyn Green. In it she writes, "If we are Christians who believe God is sovereign over all, we can believe that our assigned role as military wife has been entrusted to us by God. We can squander the opportunities that come with this assignment or, as a good steward, we can make the most out of them for the glory of God. We are in a unique position to minister to our husbands, our children, and other military families" (Green 2009, 113).

Esther was not a victim of her circumstances, and neither am I. Esther became a good steward with what she was given and ultimately saved a nation. Just as Esther did not foresee becoming queen, I never foresaw this life for myself. Christ saw fit to set me among Army wives who desperately need to be shown His love. I can sit and sulk that my husband is not physically by my side in this endeavor, or I can hold on to the call Christ has put on my life and serve those He brings my way.

The problem with bitterness and self-pity is that they lead to unhappiness, which then makes us vulnerable. Blaise Pascal, philosopher and mathematician, wrote, "All men seek happiness. This is without exception. Whatever different means they employ, they all tend to this end. The cause of some going to war, and of others avoiding it, is the same desire in both, attended with different views. The will never takes the least step but to this object. This is the motive of every action of every man, even of those who hang themselves" (Pascal n.d.).

As believers in Christ, we should be reaching for the joy that only comes from the peace of God. No matter what the trial or situation, if we are trusting in the goodness of our Savior, joy will follow. We can ask questions, we can weep in our sorrow, but in the end we must rest in God's goodness, knowing He alone holds our tomorrows. It is the only place we will be fully comforted.

DISCUSSION QUESTIONS

1. Meditate on these words from Scripture and rest in the fact that the Lord knows what's coming. That's not to say the path will always be easy. Not at all. The journey is hard, but well worth it when we have given control to God.

- Jeremiah 29:11–13
- Proverbs 16:9
- Isaiah 55:8–9

2. Is there a moment in your life where you allowed bitterness to take over? What was the outcome?

3. Do you feel comfortable asking God why? Why or why not?

4. You may know someone who feels like Elijah did, ready to call it quits, or you may be that person. Make yourself familiar with resources for those who struggle with feelings of hopelessness. Depression, addictions, cutting, and suicidal thoughts require help. If you or someone you know is dealing with any of these, please seek out help. If you do not have someone in your immediate circle whom you can reach out to, here are a few resources:

- Veterans' Crisis Line – 1-800-273-8255, www.veteranscrisisline.net (2015)

- Living Thru Crisis—Supporting Families to prevent teen suicide, depression and addiction. There are a number of resources on this site that are not just for the teen. They focus a great deal on the military family. www.livethrucrisis.com (2015)

- IMAlive—An online chat forum with trained crisis counselors. www.imalive.org (2015)

PART 5

Reintegration! His Homecoming

CHAPTER 10

A Night with the King

IT'S FUNNY HOW EXPERIENCE BRINGS to life those stories in the Bible that we've read but never quite grasped. I have found that my time as an Army wife has helped me see and understand Scripture more fully.

Matthew 25:1–13, The Parable of the Ten Virgins and Their Lamps, has always been a source of struggle for me. I never quite understood why the bridegroom would refuse them entry. It's not the overall meaning of being prepared for Christ's return that I struggled with; it was the details of the parable itself. Really, what's wrong with being fashionably late to a party?

My husband deployed in 2009 for the first time, and as I write this, he is headed out the door again. My heart breaks when he leaves. That's the best way I can put it. From the moment he walks away from us and stands in that final formation before heading off to war, I am already planning his return. He hasn't even left yet, and I am thinking of his homecoming.

During John's first deployment, I grew weary. Exhaustion was part of my every day, and yet I never stopped preparing. John's return could occur at any time. Yes, it was scheduled from a year to the date of when he left, but nothing is ever final in the Army. An injury, a family emergency, the needs of the Army, or a military withdrawal could bring him home.

The 2009 withdrawal brought many of my friends' soldiers home in late July/early August, four months sooner than scheduled. Of our church members, John was the only one who remained an ocean away. I watched eagerly as friends welcomed home their men and anxiously awaited my own phone call. It soon became apparent that John's job was not yet done, and he would serve out the remainder of his year.

We are not told the exact date or time of our spouses' return. We are given a window, which will change. Then the day comes when we are given a time—which could and often does change.

Sleep did not come easily that last month. Everything I did, from scrubbing baseboards to losing those last few pounds to buying new outfits for me and the kids to stuffing our fridge with his favorites, was all in preparation of his return. The idea that I would become complacent and not do everything possible to welcome him home was absurd and offensive. No matter how tired I became, the forefront of my thoughts was on our reuniting.

I have heard so many horror stories of men returning from war without their wives being there to greet them, only to arrive home and discover an empty house or changed locks.

Now when I read Matthew 25:1–13, there are so many layers to chew on. The five wise virgins who brought enough oil are not unlike the military spouses who keep "the home fires burning." The women in the story and the wives surrounding me eagerly await the bridegrooms return. They are respecting and honoring the men they await by being prepared at any hour. The five foolish virgins are not prepared, because they are thinking only of their immediate needs and expect the bridegroom's return on their time schedule. Suddenly the meaning of the passage found in verse 13—to stay alert because we do not know the day or the time of Christ's return—has become alive to me.

I eagerly await my Father in heaven's return, and though I do not know the day or the hour, I prepare as if it could be any moment. It is not about whether or not He will return in my lifetime. It is about showing the One Man who gave His life for me that I value, respect, and honor Him. It is about preparing my heart, and though at times I may grow weary, every moment I am aware that He could return now and I want to be ready. As I continue to grow in my understanding of Scripture and of God's amazing love, I use those gifts to share with others. It is my hope that my journey encourages others to walk more closely with God and commit more fully to their husbands.

The question is this: how will you use God's blessings and calling on your life to further His work here on earth?

Isaiah 35 speaks of rejoicing, of parched desert land that breaks forth in blooms. It speaks to fearful hearts and shaky knees, it says to stand strong because our Savior is coming. There is great anticipation and joy at the thought of our God returning to right the wrongs and to free us from suffering. Joy will replace sorrow, and we will celebrate.

The feeling when I first see my husband after a deployment is like none other. My chest is in my throat, and it takes every ounce of self-respect to keep from plowing down the people in front of me when those doors open and the smoke and soldiers pour through. My eyes scan desperately for a man I can't believe is really home until I see him and place my hand in his, a man that a hundred or more times in the last year I lay in bed terrified I would never see again. And suddenly, he is there.

Those first few days and weeks, sometimes even months, we can't keep our hands off each other. Mundane tasks like grocery shopping become family outings. The idea of being apart is absurd. We want to breathe the same air, eat off the same plate, take up the same space. It's a honeymoon all over again.

Esther prepared for a year to go to her king's bedchambers for one night. Following her one night, "She would not go back to the king unless the king was pleased with her and she was requested by name" (Esther 2:14b NET). The anticipation and fear that led to that one encounter with the king must have seemed unbearable at times.

Though my husband had chosen me many years before and had continued to choose me again and again throughout our years and struggles together, I would be lying if I said that the days leading up to our reunion are without fear. Nerves get the better of me. A lot happens in a year. I know he will be different. I know that I am different. Will he still want me? Will he still desire me? Will he still choose me again and again?

DISCUSSION QUESTIONS

1. Did you and your spouse have a honeymoon? If so, where did you go?

2. Do you remember the emotions you felt on your wedding day? Leading up to it?

3. What are you feeling now as you prepare for your spouse's return? Are you ready? Will you be ready?

4. What are you doing in your life to prepare for Christ? If He suddenly showed up and asked something big of you, would you be ready?

CHAPTER 11

When the Honeymoon Is Over

THE KING HAD NOT CALLED for Esther in 30 days . . .

I can't even imagine my husband choosing not to see me for an entire month. Even when he was deployed, thanks to technology, we never went more than a week or two without speaking. Scripture does not tell us why the king had not called for her, just that he had not. For some reason, the king did not seem to be "in love" with his queen. The newness and the honeymoon were over. Because of this, with tragedy looming, Esther had to go before her king uninvited.

Esther discovered something wonderful when she approached. Though her actions could have caused her death (Xerxes had removed the previous queen for not adhering to his authority in the presence of others), Esther discovered Xerxes still held her close to his heart. When she approached, he pardoned her life and graciously accepted an invitation to dine with her, not once but twice. When she shared what was troubling her, he believed her without question, and when he thought another man sought to physically harm her, he immediately disposed of him to protect his queen. I do not believe that the king's silence meant that Esther had in fact fallen out of favor with the king. Oftentimes I mistake my husband's silence as anger or indifference when in fact he's trying to work out something completely unrelated to us.

In *Much Ado About Loving*, Jack Murnighan evaluates the relationship of the Bagnets in Charles Dickens's novel *Bleak House*. Mr. Bagnet yearly makes a serious blunder of his wife's birthday dinner, and yet Dickens writes, "she keeps her state with all imaginable cheerfulness." Murnighan's response is heartfelt and true:

"I've always thought that the key to a relationship lasting is being able to trust that the other person loves us, and thus when he torches the chickens, shows up late, forgets an anniversary, or flies off the handle, we are capable of remembering that he's not doing it to hurt us and that something else must be at play. He's weak, he's struggling, he's unhappy, but he loves us and is probably still trying in whatever way he can. And if we help him, hold him, and, most important, don't take it personally, then we can get through the moment with all parties seeing that the love and commitment can handle a few road bumps. We might even conclude that we really are right for each other" (Murnighan 2012, 190).

As wonderful as a honeymoon period is, it is not sustainable. We all need our space. After weeks of breathing down each other's necks, a little alone time is good for each of us. When one begins to pull away from the other first is when it becomes more difficult. However, a need to reintegrate into life, to readjust to American culture and norms, requires space. It is not an indication that one spouse does not love the other. Only that both spouses need to find a new normal. We hold tightly to that promise of "till death do us part." We replay our own commitment that, no matter the circumstances, we will hold on, and we hold tight to our spouse's promise to do the same. "A promise must be about things that I can do, about actions: no one can promise to go on feeling in a certain way. He might as well promise never to have a headache or always to feel hungry" (Lewis 2002, 92).

The honeymoon period is the perfect opportunity to remind each of us why we fell in love in the first place. It allows us to reconnect, to find a peace with what has been lost, and to refocus on what has been gained. There is a new normal that has to be discovered. C.S. Lewis wrote on the commitment of love vs. being in love:

"But, of course, ceasing to be 'in love' need not mean ceasing to love. Love in this second sense—love as distinct from "being in love"—is not merely a feeling. It is a deep unity, maintained by the will and deliberately strengthened by habit; reinforced by (in Christian marriages) the grace which both partners ask, and receive, from God. They can have this love for each other even at those moments when they do not like each other; as you love yourself even when you do not like yourself . . . "Being in love" first moved them to promise fidelity: this quieter love enables them to keep the promise. It is on this love that the engine of marriage is run: being in love was the explosion that started it" (Lewis 2002, 93-94).

A new chapter of our lives has started. The honeymoon is important to reintroduce each of us to each other. I have changed over the last year of being alone with the children, the bills, the day to day, and the fear. I have learned to manage our household on my own, to parent on my own, and to be on my own. Hopefully I have grown. John has also changed in ways I cannot even begin to comprehend. He was at war for a year. No one comes home unchanged from that.

Marriage is not about feeling in love. Those moments when my soldier walks through the smoke and returns to me, the moment our eyes first meet, the moment we are lying in each other's arms for the first time in a year, are pure joy. These moments are intense, but unsustainable. They are shooting stars, fireworks, exhilarating, and thrilling. But when morning comes, they are not the moments we cling to in order to remain committed to one another.

Marriage is the privilege of being united with my best friend. It is the promise that, no matter what comes in life, I will have a partner by my side and his hand in mine. We may not agree, we may fight and have strong words for each other, but in the end, we will never let go. We will hold on tight, whatever may come.

It is a struggle to readjust, to let him take out the trash and make the grocery list. It takes a few weeks, sometimes months, to remember to ask his opinion on my social calendar. Each time he leaves, it seems that this process of reintegrating our lives takes a little longer than the time before. While he is gone, I have become selfish. My schedule is mine, my kids are mine, and my house is mine. When he returns, my language and my thoughts have to realign from *mine* to *ours*.

Marriage is a selfless act. It is continuing to place another's needs and happiness before your own. I don't mean to say that you should lose yourself; I only mean to say that when you love and honor your husband, his happiness and well-being should always be on your mind. Marriage is not about what I can do to make me happy. Marriage is a commitment to live my life with and for another. The simple things that I have changed to bring comfort in his absence need to be changed with him in mind. Here are a few of our adjustments:

- I love garlic, and we eat a ton of it while he is gone. Garlic gives him migraines and is eliminated from our diet when he is home.
- We have one car, which is never a problem during deployments. I love the freedom. I dread sharing the vehicle when he returns, and I need to attempt to complain less about my loss of freedom.
- I love to always be doing, going, visiting, or exploring. He loves to sit at home and relax in the quiet, surrounded by only his family.
- I enjoy having control over the menu. My soldier loves to cook.

I could go on, but you get the point. Things can't stay the way they are and see all of us remain happy. It's not just about my comfort. This is his home, and I am at my happiest when he is content. So together we talk, we listen, and we struggle to find a new normal together.

DISCUSSION QUESTIONS

1. What are some habits or responsibilities you acquired during your time apart that were not a part of your home prior?

2. Your spouse has changed in the last year. Changed tastes, habits, routines. How will you make a point to ask what he or she needs and then listen?

3. What are some adjustments that need to be made for your spouse to feel welcome at home? Make a list and then beginning at the top to implement one new adjustment every day until they become your new normal.

CHAPTER 12

The Real Esther Project

THE *AH-HA* MOMENT WHEN JOHN and I were watching *One Night with the King* wasn't an idea I randomly came up with. It was a desire God placed in my heart to help women, and myself, with the difficult mission of being left behind. God did not only call our husbands to serve this nation. We are serving right along with them. Our support role is vital to their well-being on the battlefield. John loved the idea of me taking a year to pamper myself and prepare myself for him. Why? Because it was my way of saying I'm waiting for you; you are worth it. To him, it was knowing that I was okay, taking moments for myself. No, The Esther Project didn't turn out like I expected. It became something richer, deeper, and more than surface level. I learned along the way the importance of taking care of myself, not just for John, but also for myself and, more importantly, for Christ. When I take the time to relax, rejuvenate, eat healthy, exercise, set boundaries, stay in God's Word, strengthen my marriage, love my children, and shower regularly, then in that moment, "for such a time as this," when God does call me to act, I am ready. My body is not my own. It has been built specifically for a mission God has called me to. One that I do not yet see clearly but that He reveals little by little. Part of that mission, though, is very clear—to love my soldier, and only him, to love him unconditionally with all my heart, respect him for who he is, and support him in the mission he has been called to.

Although I did not realize it at the time, God had started me on the Real Esther Project on November 21, 2009. It wasn't a year of lavender baths, pools of rose petals, massages, and facials (though I did fit in one pedicure). I didn't hit my weight loss goals, and the calluses on my feet and hands only grew thicker. What changed was my heart. And no, it didn't grow softer; it grew closer to God and more open to His calling. It became more willing to be a small note in a much larger orchestra of His perfect planning.

Like Esther, and more than likely like you, I grew up with a much different perspective of who I would one day become. Esther was a Jewish orphan. She probably dreamed of leading a normal life, marrying a normal Jewish husband, and having normal Jewish children. Perhaps she even had dreams of returning to Israel and rebuilding, as many of her people were doing. Even if her daydreams took her to being Queen of Persia, she never could have imagined being the one person, a Jewess orphan, who stood between her people's salvation and annihilation.

God calls ordinary people to do some overwhelmingly difficult tasks.

Abraham was told to leave everyone he knew, travel to a land he didn't know with his infertile wife, have a child at 100 years of age with that same wife, and believe God's promises, which wouldn't be fulfilled for hundreds of years.

Moses was told to take a bunch of fussy Israelites and make them wander through a desert for forty years while enduring their complaints so that their children could enter the Promised Land, the land promised to Abraham hundreds of years earlier. All the while, God was using that time to teach the Israelites to rely solely on Him, trusting Him completely for their provisions.

Hosea was commanded by God to retrieve and reunite with his unfaithful wife, Gomer. And Hosea did. All to show the Israelites how God faithfully chases after them even though they continue to turn to false gods.

Job has everything taken from him—his children, riches, and health—and never curses God. All because God wanted to prove to Satan that Job was the most righteous man on earth, simultaneously showing us who is ultimately in control.

The Real Esther Project came in the form of questions. Interestingly enough, they presented themselves in a sermon outline on Genesis 24. David Turner, Senior Pastor of Sunrise Baptist Church in El Paso, TX, was preaching on the responsibility of Abraham's senior servant and the great task Abraham placed on him by sending him back to their hometown to find a wife for his son Isaac (Turner n.d.). The questions below are adapted to fit Esther and our lives as well.

Will you promise God to do something big for Him? The task that lay before Esther was insurmountable. In order to plead for her people, she must break the law of Susa and approach the king unsummoned. The discipline that had been brought down on the former queen lay heavy on Esther. Yet the survival of her people was of greater importance than her own life. During this time of separation, is God asking something of you that feels too big? Perhaps it is simply the waiting, the remaining faithful. Perhaps the loneliness feels like it is more than you can bear. Why has God placed you "in such a time as this," and what vision does He have for the kingdom that only through your experience can be achieved? If you do not know, approach Him. Ask. Wait patiently for His answer.

Will you follow through? Are you willing to respond when He does reveal His plans to you? Will you be like Esther, who risked her own life to follow through?

When God gives you a project, do you make proper preparation, or do you wing it? Esther called on all of her people to fast with her for three days before going before the king. If God has given you a project, seek His guidance in the facilitation. Then continue to seek His guidance throughout the mission He has given you.

When you ask for leading, do you hesitate to move forward when He provides it? Esther did not have time to wait. Her people's lives were at stake. Often we do not understand or see the urgency of a project that God has given us. Remember these words of Mordecai to Esther: "For if you remain silent at this time, relief and deliverance will arise for the Jews from another place and you and your father's house will perish. And who knows whether you have not attained royalty for such a time as this?" (Esther 4:14 NASB). If God wants something done, then it is a blessing that He has asked you or me. If we stall or procrastinate, He is more than capable of finding someone more willing.

Are you hesitant to share your mission with others? The fear of death did not stop Esther from approaching the king. What is stopping you?

Do you tell others how God has answered your prayers? Do you give God credit? How does your service bless God? Because if you aren't and if it doesn't, then are you really seeking God's will, or are you seeking your own?

CHAPTER 13

The Journey Continues

IN SOME OF MY WORST nightmares, I am alone. Fear of living consumes me, and I become a fat old hermit who swats at dreams like flies. Instead of reaching for my goals, I, in the worst of nightmares, am just remaining, staying. I become nothing more than who I am today.

In some of my best dreams, there are ten of me. I climb the stairs to my flat in Italy where my three green-eyed children and my doctor wait. I study, I sleep, and I start dreams. In the summer we travel. Safari through the Garden of Eden and Kenya, tour castles throughout Europe, snorkel off Australia, trace ancestors in Ireland, Eskimo kiss in Alaska, dream of America in Boston, and so on. I will write, travel, and never stop studying. In my best dreams, I never stop evolving into the vision of me.

I wrote that little bit, which has haunted me daily since, nearly ten years ago. Dreaming is not my only nemesis. I am a planner. When I dream, I plan. Minute details plague the path from point A to point B and on and on to point Z. I am nothing like the person who wrote that little bit ten years ago. My life has not turned out to be the dream I dreamed then. It is richer, more involved, and gritty.

As I write this today, I am fighting depression. I am surrounded by books on love and happiness: *The Happiness Project, Stumbling on Happiness, Secrets to a Lasting Love*. Yet, I feel despair. Military life, cancer, and death have taught me one thing: tomorrow is uncertain. I'm grieving for friends who are losing their fight to cancer, for soldiers who are not returning home to their families, and for the upcoming deployment looming over our own heads. I feel as if I barely survived the last deployment, and now I'm looking down the barrel of a second, much more frightening prospect. The name makes me shudder. It makes me think of Harry Potter's "he who must not be named," for the whisper of it fills my heart with dread for those lost and those who will be lost. It is full of needless death. And my husband is marching into it.

For all my planning as I struggled through mounds of theological texts in seminary, for all my dreaming as I read Jane Austen and Faulkner in college, for all my hopes as I patiently sat the bench in high school, I never saw my life here. And yet I would not change the direction of it.

My flat in Italy has turned into a rock-filled yard in the midst of the El Paso desert. Our safaris are along the dry Rio Grande river bed. My husband, who once dreamed of becoming a doctor, is a soldier, and our travels occur in the form of PCS'ing and deployments.

I am struggling with my grief simply because it is hard not to swat at dreams. I am a planner. By now I should know that there is no such thing as my schedule. And yet I continue to trick myself. No first day of school, he won't be here for a single birthday, no Halloween, no Thanksgiving, no Christmas. Such is the life. And still. Still I am so grateful.

In the midst of my own pain, I am watching a dear friend and coworker struggle with her husband's fight with cancer. A fight he is quickly losing. Another friend is burying her husband. And still there is a victory in the midst as friends who celebrate being cancer free along with my own daughter. It has been an emotional few weeks. I am so blessed and yet so deeply hurt all at once.

What I yearn for right now is to sit down with my grandmother who lost a fiancé to World War II and nearly lost my grandfather. I wish to sit with her over a cup of coffee or maybe a pitcher of margaritas and just ask her, "How did you survive?" But it's too late for that. It is so true we do not know the blessings we have until they are taken from us. Oh, how I wish for her strength and her secrets that she took to the grave.

Surprisingly, it is not in the books on happiness and love that I find solace now. I find comfort from words like that of Corrie ten Boom, from *The Hiding Place*, who said:

"Worrying is carrying tomorrow's load with today's strength—carrying two days at once. It is moving into tomorrow ahead of time. Worrying doesn't empty tomorrow of its sorrow, it empties today of its strength."

I find strength from this quote by Benjamin Franklin: "Never leave that till tomorrow which you can do today" and "Trouble knocked at the door, but, hearing laughter, hurried away." I cannot let a day pass without enjoying the moment, because tomorrow may not be here. I cannot put off telling a loved one what they mean to me, for tomorrow they may not be here. I cannot put my focus onto tomorrow. I must emotionally live for today while any preparations for tomorrow, though important, may only be dreams. God knows the future. I do not. Today's strength is sufficient, and I will not be robbed of the joy of my husband's touch today for an abstract tomorrow that will come no matter how I fight it. Today I choose strength, today I choose God's grace, today I choose hope, today I choose to only see the joy in the future and let the Lord handle the details. "As for me, I will always have hope" (Psalm 71:14 NIV).

Each day I want to awake in the morning and lie down at night knowing that today . . . today was and is a good day.

Not long ago, a young woman sat in my office and shared with me some of her struggles in an overseas assignment. In a particular city, each house was surrounded by a large wall. As she walked down the street, she felt caged in, trapped, needing desperately to get out of the city but without the means to do so. A colleague gifted her with a list of all the Bible verses she could find where walls are mentioned. As she read the verses, the walls that loomed on either side of her took on a new meaning. Instead of trapping her, they represented God's protection and presence. They reminded her of the walls of the New Jerusalem found in Revelations. They no longer make her feel trapped; instead they have become a reminder of God's promises.

Deployment is like those walls. We can view deployment as a barrier to our dreams, a division in our marriages, and we can succumb to feelings of being trapped and isolated. It does not have to be that way. Instead, we can find a way to praise God for deployments. We can thank Him for the time we are given to focus more on Him, for the reminder of how precious our spouses are, and the strength God has given us to wait.

We can hold tightly to our spouse's hand while it is still in ours, cling to the memory and longing of it while an ocean away, and anticipate with joy the day we will hold it again. May you always hold on tightly and never let go.

Bibliography

Bradstreet, Anne and Hopkins, Frank Easton. *The Poems of Mrs. Anne Bradstreet (1612-1672): Together with Her Prose Remain.* The Duodecimos, 1897.

Clairmont, Patsy and Johnson, Barbara. *Outrageous Joy.* Grand Rapids, MI: Zondervan, 1999.

Diamond, Stuart. *Getting More: How You Can Negotiate to Succeed in Work and Life.* New York, NY: Crown Business, 2012.

Green, Jocelyn. *Faith Deployed: Daily Encouragement for Military Wives.* Chicago, IL: Moody Publishers, 2009.

Kendrick, Alex and Stephen. *The Love Dare.* Nashville, TN: B&H Books, 2009.

Lewis, C. S. *The Complete C.S. Lewis Signature Collection.* New York, NY: Harper Collins Publishers, 2002.

Manion, Jeff. *The Land Between: Finding God in Difficult Transitions.* Grand Rapids, MI: Zondervan, 2010.

McCullough, Donald W. *The Trivialization of God: The Dangerous Illusion of a Manageable Deity.* Navpress Publishing Group, 1995.

Murnighan, Jack and Kelly, Maura. *Much Ado About Loving: What Our Favorite Novels Can Teach You About Date Expectations, Not So-Great Gatsbys, and Love in the Time of Internet Personals.* New York, NY: Free Press, 2012.

Pascal, Blaise. n.d. *SECTION VII: MORALITY AND DOCTRINE.* Edited by W.F. Trotter. Accessed April 17, 2015. http://www.leaderu.com/cyber/books/pensees/pensees-SECTION-7.html.

One Night With the King. Directed by Michael O. Sajbel, 2006.

Turner, David. n.d. "Example of a Faithful Servant - Genesis 24." *Bible Guy.* Accessed April 17, 2015. http://bibleguy.org/sermon-resources/powerpoints/genesis/example-of-a-faithful-servant-genesis-24/12/11/).

Yancey, Phillip. *The Jesus I Never Knew.* Grand Rapids, MI: Zondervan, 2002.

For more information about

Hope N. Griffin

and
*Finding Joy: The Year Apart That Made Me
A Better Wife*

please visit:

www.HopeNGriffin.com
Hope@HopeNGriffin.com
@HopeNGriffin
www.facebook.com/HopeNGriffin

For more information about
AMBASSADOR INTERNATIONAL
please visit:

www.ambassador-international.com
@AmbassadorIntl
www.facebook.com/AmbassadorIntl